Strings, Ropes, and Cables

By Carol Krueger

Illustrated by Gaston Vanzet

Rigby

This is a piece of string.
    It does not look very strong.

 But if it's twisted into a rope...

... you can use it to go waterskiing!

Waterskiing is fun. You put skis on your feet and you hold on to a rope that is pulled by a boat.

And if you don't like water, you can take the rope...

…and attach it to a dogsled!

In very cold countries where there is a lot of snow, people travel on sleds.

Dogs are used to pull the sleds. The dogs are attached to the sleds with long ropes.

 And if you don't like snow, you can take the rope…

... and help clean windows!

The windows of very tall buildings have to be cleaned on the outside. This job is done by window cleaners.

Window cleaners sit on a platform and pull on very strong ropes to move the platform up and down.

This is a piece of wire.
　It does not look very strong.

 But if it is twisted into a cable...

… you can use it to control an elevator!

Elevators take people from one floor to another in a tall building.

Cables, pulleys, and an electric motor are used to control the elevator.

 And if you want to lift heavy loads, you can take the cable…

...and use it on a crane!

A crane is a machine that lifts and shifts heavy loads.

A crane winds a cable around a drum to lift a load and unwinds the cable to let the load down again.

 If you want to go sightseeing, you can take the cable...

…and use it to control a cable car!

Cable cars are great for going up mountains. Each car holds on to a cable.

The cable is turned by an electric motor and two huge wheels.

You can even wind up the cable…

...and use it to launch a glider!
First the cable is stretched out.

Then the winch winds the cable in very quickly.
This pulls the glider forward and up into the air.

Strings help us move in many
different ways. Some of them
are shown here.

How many can you find?